IMAGES
of England
MARYPORT

Local bicycle riders getting into their positions in 1898, ready to race on the old grass cycle track at the Cricket Ground on the Mealpot. Note that the bikes have no brakes, but have fixed wheels with wooden rims. The riders, from left to right, are: Heslop ('Eppie') Nutsford, hairdresser, of Maryport; Dick Tiffin, miner, of Dearham; Cliff Thompson, ironmonger, of Maryport; and William Baxter, cycle maker, of Maryport.

Cover illustration: Doctor John W. Crerar of 11 High Street at the wheel of his 1902 $3\frac{1}{2}$hp Swift car. It is thought to have been the first car in Maryport and was capable of 20mph flat out over a short distance. In 1903 cars had to be registered and this car was given the number AO40. The car is seen here leaving Birkby Green. With Dr Crerar is Claude Mann, who was his chauffeur for fifty-five years.

IMAGES
of England

MARYPORT

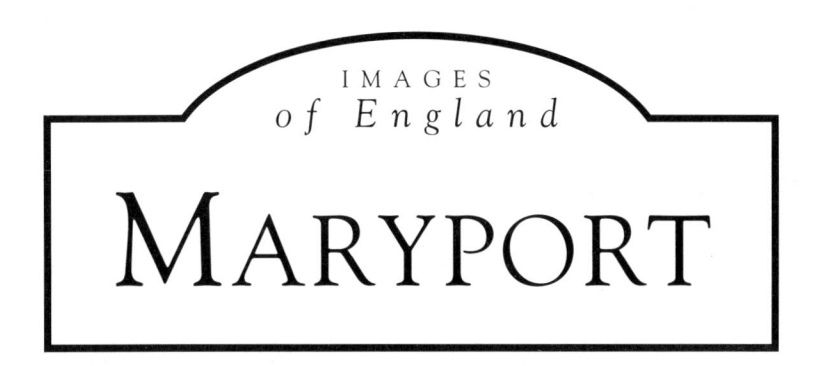

Compiled by
Keith Thompson

TEMPUS

First published 2000
Copyright © Keith Thompson, 2000

Tempus Publishing Limited
The Mill, Brimscombe Port,
Stroud, Gloucestershire, GL5 2QG

ISBN 0 7524 2158 1

Typesetting and origination by
Tempus Publishing Limited
Printed in Great Britain by
Midway Clark Printing, Wiltshire

The 2nd Maryport Boys' Brigade Company Band of the Presbyterian church, Crosby Street, c. 1910. The Boys' Brigade movement was formed in Glasgow on 4 October 1883, by William Alexander Smith, a Sunday school teacher and member of the 1st Lanarkshire Rifle Volunteers. The movement was an immediate success and quickly spread south, reaching Carlisle by 1889. Over the next few years it spread to many towns and villages in West Cumberland. The Brigade's motto was 'Sure and Steadfast'.

Contents

Acknowledgements 6

Introduction 7

1. The Docks and Harbour Area 9

2. Down Street and Bank End 37

3. Around the Town 45

4. Shops and the Town Centre 57

5. Netherhall and District 75

6. Grasslot and the Railway 89

7. Sport and Leisure 105

8. Flimby 117

Acknowledgements

I would like to thank Phil Croutch and the Maritime Museum, Maryport, and Cumbria County Council Library of Carlisle for allowing me to reproduce their photographs. Thanks to Kathleen Wallace for her help and for giving me the opportunity to use part of her Senhouse collection. I am indebted to Sydney Logan and the large number of friends and acquaintances around Maryport, too numerous to mention, who also have allowed me to copy their photographs. Without their contribution this book would not have been possible.

I would also like to give thanks to Lloyd and Louise Thompson for all their help, and most of all to my wife Jean, who started our collection of postcards and photographs; it is her enthusiasm that has made this collection materialize.

A group of local miners after a shift at the coal-face, c. 1908. These men are pit deputies, responsible for the miners' safety and for measuring how much coal had been dug, for which they used the rods they are holding. They are wearing knee-length moleskin trousers, the traditional hard-wearing clothes popular with miners at this time.

Introduction

The collection of photographs and postcards which you are about to view has been carefully selected to depict Maryport's social scene over a period of approximately 150 years. The earliest picture dates from around 1815 and the latest from 1963. Many of the pictures have been obtained from private collections of friends and family, to whom I'm eternally grateful. We have spent many hours discussing the historical and social background of each individual scene. As everyone knows, 'every picture tells a story', but that story can be interpreted differently by each and every one of you, when you conjure up your own memories from it.

The majority of the postcards chosen to feature in this book are dated between 1904 and 1918, which was the peak period for postcard production, with most households owning a postcard album. The invention of the telephone and installation of telephone exchanges in Maryport and its surrounding district revolutionized communication over long distances. Thereafter, the market for postcards shifted to tourists; they were mass-produced and featured mainly the landscape around Maryport.

Maryport's economic history has undoubtedly shaped its social history. There follows a brief history of Maryport as a background to the industrial expansion the town went through during the eighteenth and nineteenth centuries.

Maryport was a planned town and was firmly established on the map by the middle of the eighteenth century. It was named by Humphrey Senhouse of Netherhall, who also instigated the rise in prosperity through industrialization. Archives shows that from 1750, when it was noted that only the second house in Maryport had been built, the town expanded rapidly; it had 12,000 registered inhabitants by the beginning of the twentieth century.

Industry flourished, mainly through the opening of the Elizabeth Dock in 1857 and the Senhouse Dock in 1884, and also the Maryport & Carlisle Railway in 1845. Maryport's harbour was principally founded on the export of coal to Ireland; however, other exports included steel rails, stone, lime, bar bolts and cast iron, all of which came from works established in Maryport and outlying districts, such as the Solway Iron Works and the collieries based in Ellenborough, Flimby, Dearham and Aspatria. Shipbuilders' yards were a common sight, with Maryport offering the largest docks on the West Cumbria coastline until 1927, when the Prince of Wales Dock opened at Workington. From this point onwards, industry around the harbour began to decline, with new production industries moving into the town, particularly around the area of Grasslot, where several factories were built and employed many local people.

As a matter of course, as Maryport's industries flourished so did the social life of its inhabitants. By the turn of the nineteenth century, Maryport boasted some thirty-seven hotels, taverns and beer-houses, numerous clubs and societies were formed and various celebrities of the era stayed in the town centre. The Golden Lion Hotel in Senhouse Street played host to Charles Dickens, Wilkie Collins and George Stephenson, to name but a few.

The structure of the book and the sequence of photographs are not chronological, and my intention is not to write a comprehensive history of the town but to offer a glimpse into the lives of its inhabitants. Pictures of various social events and incidents, which have occurred over the 150 years covered, have been divided into geographical areas of the town. The book starts with a chapter on the docks and harbour area, and the following chapters will take you on a tour around Maryport and its outlying districts, ending at Flimby.

Three schooners laden with coal being towed out of the harbour into the Solway Firth by one of the Maryport tugboats, *c.* 1895.

One
The Docks and Harbour Area

This print from around 1816 shows the wooden piers built to form the harbour at the mouth of the River Ellen. Prior to this, small ships had to sail into the mouth of the river to load coal, which was brought down from the local pits in panniers on the backs of ponies. The construction of the piers enabled coal to be loaded much more easily, especially at low water when coal could be dropped straight into the hulls. At this time Maryport was a base for a small fleet of fishing boats. Herring were plentiful and were sold by the barrel, preserved in salt and eaten over the coming months.

Looking down onto the piers and quays from the rear yard of the Golden Lion on Shipping Brow. By the 1830s coal was transported to the harbour by teams of horses and carts from the pits. In 1843 an Admiralty survey and report on the West Cumberland ports recommended the formation of a wet dock and the extension of the piers to accommodate the increased shipping.

This print of 1815 looks across the River Ellen towards Mote Hill and Paper Mill Green. Travellers and packhorses used the bridge across the river on the left; this was the main route from West Cumberland to Carlisle. In the eighteenth century a paper mill had been built on this site which only worked for a few years. Eventually the site was leased by Issac Middleton as a shipbuilding yard, which itself closed in the 1860s.

William Mitchell's painting of the graving bank and bridge in 1834. The scene shows cattle swimming ashore onto the bank after being driven overboard. Castle Hill, the dower house of the Senhouse family, can be seen in the background on top of Mote Hill. Beyond the bridge a ship stands on the stocks of Ritson's shipyard.

The South Quay in February 1900 with the Ship Inn, which is now the Navy Club.

The Senhouse Dock and dock basin under construction. Mrs Elizabeth Pocklington Senhouse of Netherhall cut the first sod in February 1880. The dock extends to six acres in area.

Contractors working on the gates to the new dock, c. 1883.

The opening of the Senhouse Dock on 27 May 1884, when the Hine Brothers' vessel *Alne Holme* took Mrs Senhouse and her guests aboard on the North Quay. The ship left the harbour and was followed by a flotilla of small boats out into the Solway Firth. This shows the *Alne Holme* after returning to port, approaching the dock gates with the naval reservists standing on the yard-arms. As she passed through the gates, breaking a thin ribbon, Mrs Senhouse who was on the bridge declared the dock open.

The *Lynton*, a steel four-masted barque of 2,531 tons, being towed out of Maryport by the tug *Sarah Jolliffe* in Nov 1901. She was laden with steel rails bound for Chanaral in Chile.

The figurehead from the barque *Mary Ann Johnston* built at Maryport in 1848. James Brooker of Eaglesfield Street was the carver. James had arrived in Maryport around 1840; he was a native of Liverpool and by 1851 he was married with six children. He employed one man and was listed as a master ship's carver. He left Maryport shortly after this date.

The south pier, looking towards the lighthouse, was built in 1846 and shows the red tide float. This was raised and lowered depending on the tide, to let shipping know when the water was deep enough to enter the harbour. Before the float a flag was used as a signal.

A group of blacksmiths and fitters outside their workshop between the Elizabeth and Senhouse Docks, c. 1895. The building was part of Pearson Dodgson's business; he was a ship's chandler, engineer and blacksmith of 18 Senhouse Street.

The 707-ton *Southerfield*, the last wooden ship built by Ritson & Co., was launched in October 1881. Her dimensions were 177ft long by 33ft wide, with a draught of 19ft, and she was owned by the builders. In 1888 she was lost after catching fire off Cape Horn while laden with nitrate. All her crew were rescued unharmed by a passing ship.

The lifeboat *Henry Nixon* outside Christ Church, returning to the harbour after a tour around the streets on the occasion of the opening of the Senhouse Dock in May 1884. This vessel was replaced in 1886 by the lifeboat *Civil Service No. 5*.

The rescue of the *Estrelle de Chile* from the Robin Rigg sandbank in the Solway Firth off Maryport in 1888. The Maryport lifeboat *Civil Service No. 5* was towed towards the wreck by the tug *Senhouse*. The lifeboatmen found the crew of fourteen clinging to the masts and rigging. After eventually getting all the crew safely into the lifeboat, with the lifeboatmen and crewmen exhausted, she was again taken in tow by the *Senhouse* and arrived safely back in port.

The centre ladder dredger, which was purchased by the Maryport Harbour Commissioners in 1905, is seen clearing silt from the Senhouse Dock basin.

Robert Ritson (1810-1887) took over the running of the family's shipyard on Irish Street with his brother William, on the death of their father John in 1844. In 1851 Ritson & Co. had eight shareholders and employed 152 men and 30 boys. William died in 1866, leaving Robert in control; his two sons joined him in the business. Ritson & Co. continued to build ships until 1902 when the yard was taken over by William Walker, who continued to build ships for a number of years. After William Walker the yard traded under the name of the Maryport Shipbuilding and Repair Company.

The Senhouse dock, looking north, with ships decorated for the Coronation of George V in 1911.

A view of the Elizabeth Dock and the Liverpool-registered *Gertie* passing through the dock gates, *c.* 1915. Down the left-hand side of the dock are four hurries for loading coal from rail wagons into the ships.

The broadside launch of the *Kinkora* in September 1888. She was the largest ship built by Ritson & Co. up to that date. The order was placed by John Porter, a ship-owner of Belfast. The launch attracted a large crowd from the Maryport district, shops closed early and people made their way to the side of Mote Hill. Between seven and eight thousand people were gathered on the hillside to see the launch.

Just before one o'clock the keel blocks and props holding the ship were removed and with a bit of propulsion she started to move towards the river. Mrs John Porter, wife of the owner, named the ship *Kinkora*. As the ship hit the water and rolled, a large amount of water was displaced, which ran onto Mote Hill and caused damage to the retaining wall. The *Kinkora* was an iron sailing ship measuring 261ft by 39ft by 23ft and weighing 1,790 tons.

After the ship had settled in the river, she was towed into the Senhouse Dock where she was prepared for sailing. The *Kinkora* was in service until May 1897. She became a total wreck on a reef off Clipperton Island, 200 miles north of Acapulco, while on a voyage from Port Puget Sound, USA, to England with a cargo of timber. The crew of twenty-seven landed on the island safely.

A group of ladies on the platform at the launching ceremony of *Lycidas* in Ritson's shipyard, c. 1902.

The wreck of the schooner *Jane* of Wigtown, May 1905. She became stranded in a storm while coming into Maryport with a load of pit-wood. The lifeboat rescued the crew of three at a cost of £15 3s; the schooner became a total wreck.

The launch of the second *Civil Service No. 5* lifeboat in 1905. The Civil Service Lifeboat Fund was set up in 1866 by Post Office workers to buy a life boat for the RNLI. The fund was so well supported that it continued and is still ongoing to this day.

The new *Civil Service No. 5* with some of the townspeople aboard after its launch. She was 38ft long by 9ft 4in wide, a Watson class non-self-righter, built by the boatyard of the Thames Ironworks at a cost of £1,011. She served Maryport until 1931.

Maryport lifeboat *Priscilla MacBean* with Tommy Reay Cox, his sons Issac and William, and the rest of the crewmembers. She was a 35ft motor self-righter and came to Maryport from Kirkcudbright in 1931 and served until 1934. Walker's engineering workshop can be seen behind the lifeboat.

The launching ceremony of the *Joseph Braithwaite* by the Countess of Lonsdale in September 1934. The lifeboat was named after Joseph Braithwaite who was born in 1832 at Wigton and spent most of his life in Brighton and Hove. He died in 1882 leaving a bequest of £5,000 to the RNLI, to be given after his wife's death. This was fifty-two years later, and Maryport benefited, as it was the nearest station to his birthplace.

Looking south from North Quay towards the swing bridge across the harbour, which was built in 1835 as a toll bridge. The gridiron, where ships were moored for repairs, lies beyond.

A Maryport dredger on the gridiron in around 1908, with J. Wharton's engineers and smiths on King Street in the background. These properties were demolished in the late 1960s and the site became part of the Well Lane housing development.

25

The steam tug *Netherhall* and sailing ships in the Senhouse Dock *c.* 1903. The Maryport Harbour Commissioners had purchased the *Netherhall* when the Maryport Steam Shipping Co. went into liquidation in 1900, after operating the tugs in Maryport harbour for forty years. The *Netherhall* was scrapped in 1935.

The Commercial Buildings, South Quay, *c.* 1910. This property housed three businesses. On the left is W.E. Fisher, shipping agent and broker; in the centre is M. Greggains, which was run by Richard Thompson and Peter Greggains who were stevedores and shipping contractors; and on the right is Joseph Holmes, also a shipping agent.

Contractors demolishing the old south pier around 1939, before building the new concrete pier. The work was carried out by the construction firm Harbour and General. The original pier was built in the first half of the nineteenth century and was extended several times.

27

An engraving of Shipping Brow by the Revd R. Lawson MA in 1837, showing Ritson's sail room on the left and the Queen's Head Inn on the right. The latter building now houses the Maritime Museum.

An early twentieth-century view of Shipping Brow across the harbour, with Quintin Moore's chandlery on the left. The Queen's Head Inn, on the right, was rebuilt in 1881 and has changed little since. This building is now the Maritime Museum.

A group of dock-gate men, who were responsible for making sure the dock gates were opened and closed for the ships. They also assisted in the docking of ships.

Dock-gate man Thomas Henney with his model yacht *Heney* in front of the Elizabeth Dock gatekeepers' shelter. Thomas had been a ship's carpenter in Maryport. At the beginning of the twentieth century there was a model yacht club in Maryport.

Small herring boats in the Elizabeth Dock basin unloading their catches. A number of local families owned boats in the 1920s and '30s.

Fishing boats in the Elizabeth Docks. During the 1930s and '40s, when herring were plentiful, a large number of Scottish and Irish boats fished out of Maryport during the herring season.

Elizabeth Dock in 1899, full of boats known as 'colliers' being loaded with coal. The majority of these boats would cross to Northern Ireland. Up to sixty vessels were known to put to sea on a single tide.

The *Netherholme* berthed in the Senhouse Dock. She was built in 1888 and was the twelfth ship built by J.L. Thompson of Sunderland for Hine Bros. She weighed 1,285 tons and was 277ft long, with a crew of twenty-two, and was used to transport steel rails from the local ironworks for the Canadian Pacific Railway. In 1907 she was wrecked off the Pembrokeshire coast. She was re-floated but was then broken up in 1908.

The launch of the *Point Clear* in February 1901. She weighed 507 tons and had dimensions of 166ft by 27ft by 11ft. Steamers built in Maryport were towed to Glasgow to have their engines fitted. This added to their cost and was one of the factors that eventually led to the yard's closure.

Stevedores by the side of the Senhouse Dock.

The Ritson-built *Netherby*, an iron ship launched in May 1886 which weighed 448 tons. She was built for a Liverpool shipping company but in 1903 she was bought back by Ritson & Co. This photograph shows her leaving Maryport in June 1906 for Chile, where she was lost with all hands.

33

Contractors employed to unload cement for Thomas Mandle builders' merchants of South Quay, seen cleaning up the Cumbria shed after a shipment, c. 1927. The shed was situated on the corner of South Quay and the Elizabeth Dock basin.

Looking across from South Quay towards King Street and Christ Church. The Brow Street Methodist Chapel, which was later burned down, is visible behind Christ Church.

The view from North Quay towards South Quay and the rear of the Cumbria shed.

A small coaster leaving harbour in 1922. She is passing the Cumbria shed on the right.

Looking onto Ritson's old shipyard, *c.* 1950. Just visible on the left in the background are the chimneys and roofs of J. Wharton's Phoenix Iron Foundry.

Two
Down Street and Bank End

Looking south along King Street during floods in 1890. Nothing seems to have changed in this regard, as flooding still occurs every few years when strong winds and high tides coincide. The large building near Christ Church was the Carrs flour warehouse. When Carrs moved away from Maryport, Lakeland Foods took over the warehouse and turned it into a fruit-canning factory. They eventually moved onto the new industrial estate at Grasslot and the old factory was demolished around 1960.

The harbour entrance, with the South and North Piers. Above the roof tops is the Tongue Pier, in the centre.

Down Street, part of the core of old Maryport, which was built around the harbour in the late eighteenth and early nineteenth centuries.

The interior of Christ Church, King Street. The foundation stone was laid in January 1871 and the church was consecrated in 1873. It was restored in 1894 as a chapel of ease to St Mary's. The roof structure was designed to resemble the upturned hull of a ship.

A local character, Ben Satterthwaite, with his sewage cart at his stables. Ben was a native of Keswick and lived with his wife and family in King Street.

School dinners arriving at Christ Church Nursery, Nelson Street, in 1933. Dinners were cooked at Park House domestic science kitchen in North Street and taken down Brow Street in a bakery handcart by one of the unemployed fathers.

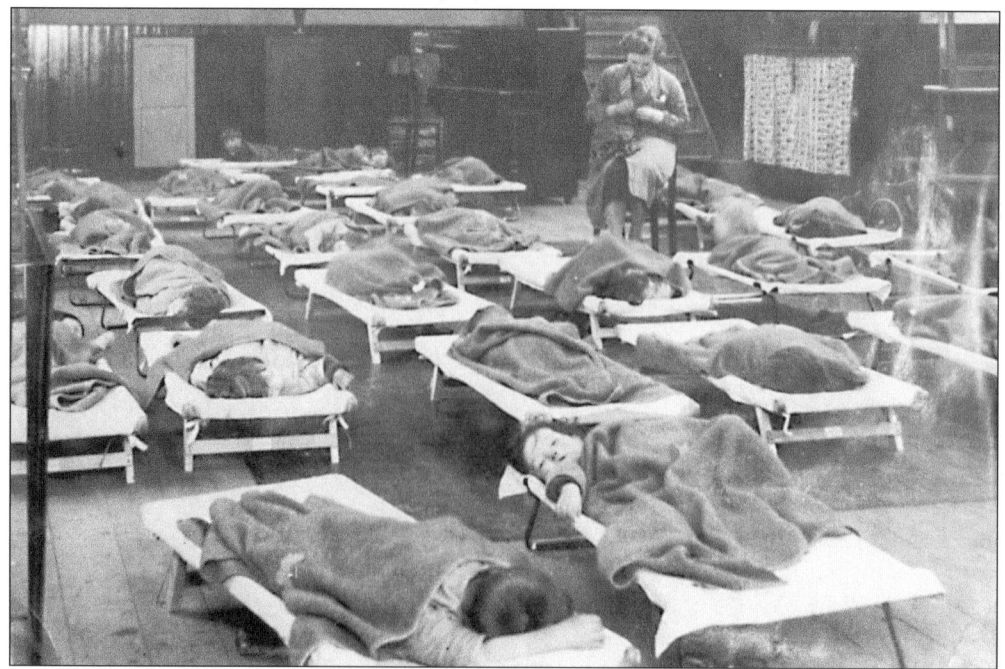

The nursery school was opened 1933 in the former Christ Church Mission, also known as the Johnson Mission Room, which was built in 1891. Miss Gladys Harvey was the first headmistress and had two assistants to help her with the children. This photograph shows the children resting on the camp beds after having lunch.

A bottle-nosed whale on the beach in front of the gasworks in September 1939. It had been found drifting in the Solway Firth by a local fishing boat, whose crew, fearing it would cause damage to their nets, decided to tow it ashore. It was 21ft long and weighed $2\frac{1}{2}$ tons, and was thought to have been killed by a steamer or a depth charge, as its flesh was torn down one side.

Looking along the finished sea wall, built to halt the erosion of the coastline. Local labour was used, as a large proportion of the workforce in Maryport had been unemployed for a number of years. It was completed in early 1939 and is $1\frac{1}{4}$ miles long.

A view of the putting green and concrete roller-skating rink, which were built by a group of local businesspeople in the late 1920s. The rink was also the venue for touring variety acts, when a stage would be erected for the concerts.

William Mitchell's painting of 1893 looking towards Bank End Farm. The ruins may have been an old tollgate, as this had been the route of the main road to Carlisle via Allonby. Near this was the site of an old salt pan owned by the Senhouse family.

Bank End Farm, *c.* 1900. This is one of the oldest properties in the area, built in 1716 by Humphrey and Elizabeth Senhouse and later becoming one of the estate farms. In the middle of the nineteenth century it was farmed with 400 acres, part of which would have been land above the shoreline which has been greatly reduced over the years by the stormy seas.

Maryport golf club, which was opened as a nine-hole course in 1905. The fairways and greens for the nine holes were on the left between top of the shore and the Allonby road.

43

Looking south towards the golf clubhouse, which was built in 1908. Previously, the club members used one of the buildings belonging to Bank End Farm as a store for their clubs and other equipment.

The salt pans near Crosscanonby. This area, one of the many up and down the Solway coast, was used for the extraction of salt by evaporation of seawater before 1800. By the early twentieth century, the site had become a park for caravans.

Three
Around the Town

Fleming Square was named after Sir George Fleming of Rydal, Bishop of Carlisle and father of Mary Senhouse, after whom Maryport was named. This photograph shows geese for sale in Fleming Square on market day. This was a common site in the markets of West Cumberland as large numbers of geese were shipped over from Ireland in the coal boats. Once ashore, geese bound for Cockermouth would be driven along the highway to the market.

Markets were held on Friday, when the local farmers would bring their produce by pony and cart to sell. The centre-covered market was built in 1875 and had replaced a smaller building, which had been built in 1850. The interior of the new market was fitted out with stalls for butter, eggs and meat; outside in the square vegetables were sold.

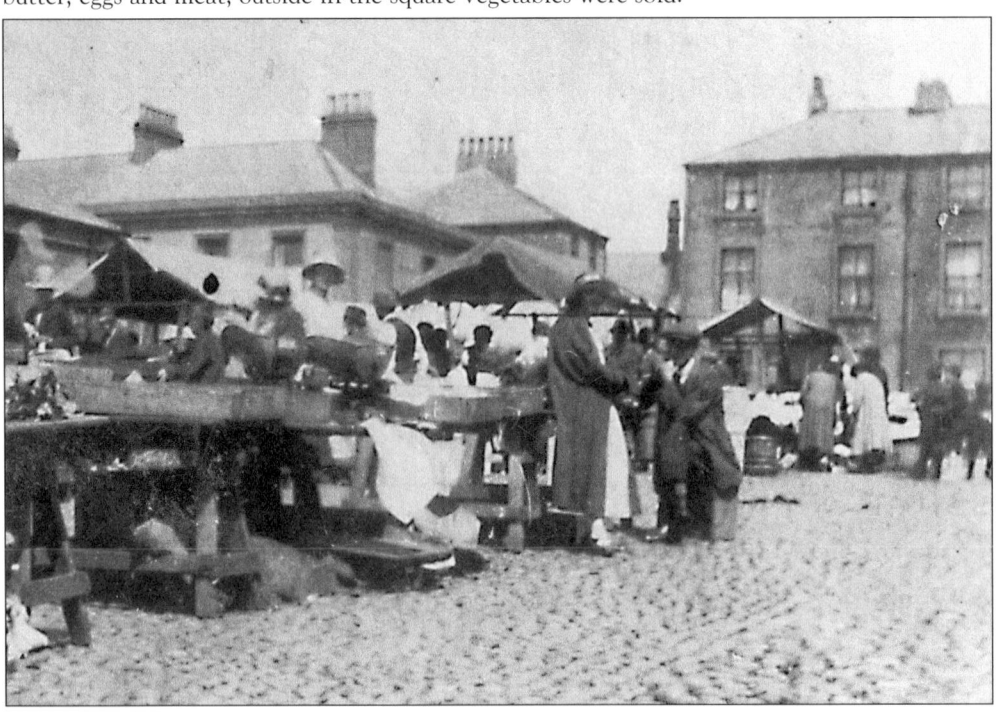

Camp Hill and Park Hill, at the top of Camp Road, were built by Wilfred and Alfred Hine, shipowners. Both men were natives of Maryport, but Wilfred had previously been involved with shipping in Liverpool. Returning to Maryport, he went into partnership with his younger brother Alfred and in 1873 they formed the Holme Line and operated from the Custom House Buildings on South Quay.

The entrance gate to Camp Hill and Park Hill decorated for the homecoming of Captain Alfred Hine Jnr from the Boer War in 1902.

47

The Royal Naval Reserve Hall (known as the 'Battery') was opened in 1886 as a centre for training naval reservists. It consisted of a drill hall, battery and one office; the battery had three heavy guns, one with a travelling carriage. Up to 200 men were trained here annually – mostly local merchant seamen and fishermen. It also housed the coastguard station, with John Mitchell as chief officer.

A group of naval reservists outside the Battery, c. 1895. They are seen with their Martini-Henry rifles and bayonets.

The British School, North Street, was built in 1883 as a mixed school to hold 465 pupils. It was destroyed by a German bomber in July 1940. The site was eventually cleared and prefabricated buildings were erected for school use. During this period the pupils of the British and National Schools amalgamated, using various properties in the town to hold lessons.

Pupils in the domestic science classroom of the British School. This was separate from the main school building and escaped serious bomb damage.

SOLWAY HOUSE.

Solway House, formerly the home of the Williamson family, who owned the tannery in Nelson Street. This property was taken over by the education authority after the war and used as a school after the British School had been bombed. Solway House was used as a mixed school until 1955 when the boys moved to the new Netherhall School built in Netherhall Park, with Mr J.W. Penn as the first headmaster. The girls followed four years later, when a new girls' school was erected alongside the boys' with Miss I. Milne as the first headmistress.

The school choir at Solway House with Mr Liverick the choirmaster, c. 1948.

A view along North Street in the 1920s. The houses on the left had their cast-iron garden railings removed by emergency powers to help the scrap metal effort in the Second World War.

Fair day in Fleming Square, c. 1935. The fair was held on Friday and Saturday of Whit weekend and the Friday and Saturday before 12 November. The travelling fair arrived in town, with roundabouts and swing-boats, as well as coconut shies and sideshows – all the fun of the fair. By the time the residents of the Square woke up on Sunday morning the fair would have gone, as the fair folk dismantled their rides during the night.

Maryport fire engine and crew near the junction of Camp Road and Christian Street, *c.* 1897. The engine was garaged in Fleming Square and the keys were kept at the police station, with a spare set at the gasworks.

The police station and magistrates' court in Eaglesfield Street, *c.* 1907. The station was built in the middle of the nineteenth century.

Crosby Street from Fleming Square, c. 1950. On the left is the Presbyterian church, which was enlarged in 1888 when two churches united. It closed in 1981 and was demolished a short time later. On the right is the Catholic church, which is dedicated to Our Lady and St Patrick.

The interior of Our Lady and St Patrick's church, which was built in 1838 and rebuilt in 1847 to provide more seating for the increasing Catholic community arriving in Maryport.

Standing on the right is William Langcake at his father's workshop at 67 Kirkby Street around 1900, with two of their workers. Thomas Langcake was a blacksmith and agricultural implement maker. William later became chief fire officer in Maryport.

Mary O'Pray with her coal cart. Mary was as strong as any man, delivering bags of coal to houses and coal cellars. On rainy days she wore a man's double-breasted topcoat with her head covered by a soft bonnet.

Members of the Salvation Army Corps outside their meeting hall in John Street, c. 1920. Their hall had previously been a Presbyterian church. The Maryport citadel of the Salvation Army was formed in 1886 and their first anniversary was held in the Athenaeum in High Street. They met in John Street for forty years until in 1928 they moved into the old Congregational church in Lawson Street.

John Sibson of Brow Street was Maryport's first letter carrier. John would be seen on his rounds wearing a long bright scarlet coat with gilt buttons. Apart from being a letter carrier John was also a bell-man, bill-poster and a cobbler. John's wife Jane also worked as a letter carrier.

The 'Maryport Nuts', c. 1914. These men enlisted at the outbreak of the First World War and became part of a West Cumberland unit which formed part of the 4th East Lancashire Howitzer Brigade, Royal Field Artillery. They are seen here at their training camp in North Wales. When their training was completed they saw action in Gallipoli, Mesopotamia (now Iraq) and, in 1916, on the Western Front.

The Golden Lion on Shipping Brow, c. 1930. This hotel was built on the site of an early farmhouse sometime in the late eighteenth or early nineteenth century, although it has been altered over the years. It was listed as an early posting inn. In 1916 it was taken over, along with the Maryport Brewery, as part of the Carlisle State Management Scheme to regulate the licensing hours and stop absenteeism from work through drunkenness.

Four
Shops and the Town Centre

The Co-operative movement opened its first shop on Senhouse Street in 1858. In 1864 they opened a shop on the corner of Wood Street and over the following years expanded along the street. Unable to develop further, they decided to look for a site on which to build a new store. Eventually Furnace Mill meadow on Curzon Street was chosen as the most suitable site. The first stores were opened in July 1883 and the whole site was completed by 1899. This photograph shows the Maryport Co-operative Industrial Society shops on Curzon Street, c. 1904.

Looking north along Curzon Street, c. 1905. This street was named after Blanche Curzon, née Senhouse, of Kedleston Hall, Derbyshire.

Curzon Street from the junction of Senhouse Street, c. 1955. The Bata shoe shop, which opened around 1950, is on the corner. The Bata shoe manufacturing company of Tilbury had built a new factory on the Solway Industrial Estate and began to manufacture shoes in 1947.

John J. Gardiner is on the left with his mechanic outside his cycle shop at 31 Curzon Street, c. 1906. John had previously run his business from 104 Senhouse Street. John was one of the first men in Maryport to own a car and charabanc.

The No. 2 Cumberland bus and crew, seen parked outside their office and waiting room at 31 Curzon Street. The Whitehaven Motor Services changed to the Cumberland Motor Services in 1921 and operated this bus on the Whitehaven to Carlisle service.

A church procession marches along Curzon Street after attending a fête in Netherhall grounds with their banner 'You May Bend The Sapling, Not The Tree'.

Looking up Senhouse Street from Curzon Street, c. 1906. This part of Senhouse Street was built on what was known as Dixon's meadow around 1880.

Maryport band, known as the 'Town Band', leading a procession down Senhouse Street during the celebrations for the Coronation of George V, 1911.

Senhouse Street in around 1955, with Robert Gordon's decorator's shop in the centre and Hird's milk bar to the left.

61

John Dixon with his youngest children, Leslie and Jane, outside his watchmakers and jewellers shop at 79 Senhouse Street. John had started in business in 1880 at 104 Crosby Street, having served his apprenticeship as a watchmaker. His father and grandfather had both been tailors at 17 Wood Street. His eldest son Norman eventually took over the business and John's grandchildren John and Mary now run the shop.

Dan Crone opened this tailor's shop at 72 Senhouse Street in 1879. Dan continued trading until 1906, when his son Tom took over. Crone & Co. traded for over a hundred years through four generations. To the immediate left of the shop is the Empire Theatre which was opened in 1911; it later became a cinema.

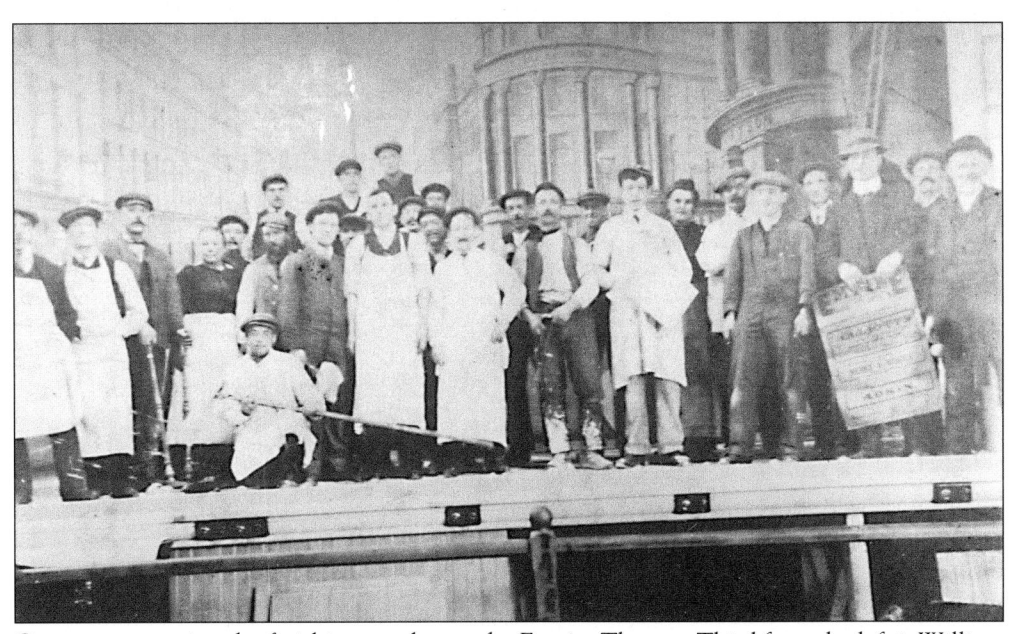

Contractors putting the finishing touches to the Empire Theatre. Third from the left is William Langcake the blacksmith, holding steel spindles for the staircase.

James Palmer (in the trilby hat) outside his wet fish shop at 64 Senhouse Street, *c.* 1901. He had recently moved from 76 Crosby Street. He also cured fish at 31 Wood Street. His two sons Jim and Reg took over the business and traded as Palmer Bros retail and wholesale fish merchants.

Senhouse Street in the 1950s. The Shakespeare Inn and Walter Wilson's store are on the right.

The junction of Senhouse Street and Crosby Street, c. 1900. On the far right corner is the London City and Midland Bank.

Looking along Crosby Street in the direction of Fleming Square, with Musgrave's drapery store on the right.

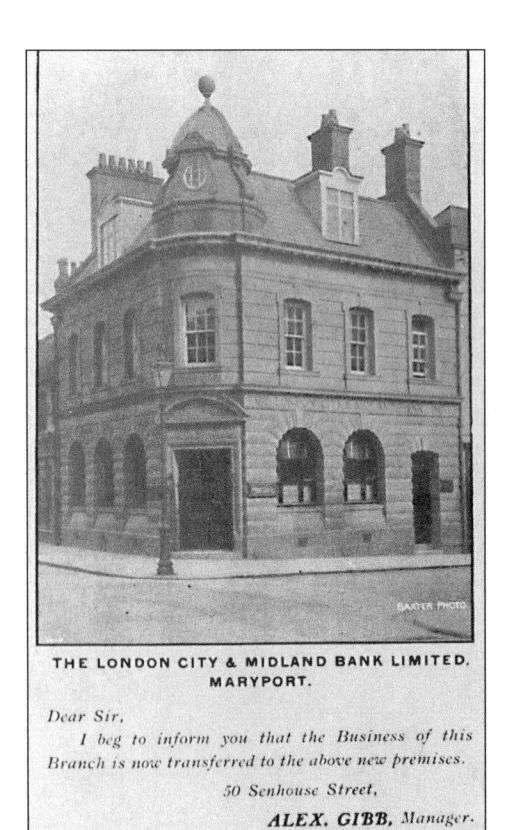

THE LONDON CITY & MIDLAND BANK LIMITED,
MARYPORT.

Dear Sir,
 I beg to inform you that the Business of this Branch is now transferred to the above new premises.
50 Senhouse Street,
ALEX. GIBB, Manager.

The recently rebuilt London City and Midland Bank, which was opened around 1906.

John Cartmer standing on the left outside his butchers' shop at 72 Crosby Street. The Cartmer family had been butchers in Maryport since the beginning of the nineteenth century. John was the son of a hairdresser on Furnace Lane.

Senhouse Street, looking towards Shipping Brow with Miss Jane Hull's tobacconist's shop at 47 Senhouse Street on the left. Further along at no. 43 is the Maryport Coffee Tavern, which was built in 1880 and became the meeting place for most of the town's societies and sports organizations.

67

Looking north along the High Street. On the left is the old post office, which later became the harbour office. On the right is the Athenaeum which was erected in 1857 to house both a Mechanics' Institute and reading rooms.

The junction of Senhouse Street and High Street, *c.* 1904. Lipton's grocers, previously W.H. Richmond, is at no. 22 Senhouse Street. The shop on the right, 41 High Street, belonged to Thomas Skelton, a chemist and dentist.

Looking along Senhouse Street from High Street in the 1920s, when a large number of Maryport men were unemployed. The building on the left, formerly the Cumberland Union Bank, was a store for local decorator James McKay. On the right can be seen the Town Hall which was built in 1890 with the clock outside.

Senhouse Street in 1952, with the Carlton Cinema on the left. This had been built as a bank, but was converted into a cinema, being opened in 1934. Further along on the left is Sandham's confectioner's van.

Joseph Newby's grocery shop was established around 1830 at 74 High Street. It was then taken over by John Temple and his son Joseph (seen in this photograph, c. 1890) followed him. The shop was well known for blending tea and roasting coffee daily. Robert Nixon continued the business after Joseph Temple retired.

Looking down High Street, c. 1911. On the right behind the billboards was Gill's market. Shortly afterwards the site was cleared to make way for the new post office and telephone exchange.

Maryport postwomen, c. 1916. They were recruited to replace the men who had gone to serve in the First World War. The first lady recruited was Faith Head of Mill Street, seen standing on the left. She began work in January 1916 and her area was Fothergill and Flimby. Every week day in all weathers, she set out on foot at 5 a.m. from the High Street with her post-bag which could weigh up to 60lb.

Confectioner Jane Dixon and staff outside her shop at 17 Wood Street. Before Jane started her business here, it had been the family tailor's shop.

Looking up Wood Street, c. 1908. Just visible on the left is the garden of the brewery manager's residence.

William Thompson (left) and his brother Clifton outside 127 Crosby Street. William had served his apprenticeship as a plumber in Altrincham, Cheshire. On returning to Maryport, he set up in business at 62 John Street. He moved to the above address in 1903. By 1908 he was in partnership with his younger brother Clifton, who had trained as an ironmonger with Mirehouse Wilson in Wood Street. They then traded as Thompson Bros.

Wood Street from Netherhall corner. On the left beyond the shops is part of the Maryport Brewery, which closed in 1921. Opposite, on the right, are Thomas Ferguson's cabinet maker's premises at 76 Wood Street.

Standing outside his shop around 1927 is Charles Over, the fifth generation of a family of watchmakers who originally came from Coventry. Charles's grandfather John had arrived in Maryport with his wife and family in 1870 and set up in business at 77 Wood Street. They then moved to 89 Wood Street in 1886 and John's two sons, Charles's father Edward and uncle Joseph began trading as watchmakers, jewellers and cycle dealers.

Five
Netherhall and District

An early painting of St Mary's chapel, which was built in 1770 as a chapel of ease to Crosscanonby church. In 1837 it was extended and a tower was added in 1847.

St Mary's church, which replaced the chapel in 1891. The chapel tower was the only part saved, although it was altered at a later date. Mrs Elizabeth P. Senhouse had the church hall (on the left) built in Church Street in 1882.

A tree-lined Netherhall Road, c. 1908. This was a popular walk for families and courting couples, especially on a Sunday evening after the church service.

Netherhall corner in around 1905, showing Ritson's grooms returning with their horses to Ellenbank.

St Mary's church and Netherhall corner after the memorial gardens were formed to commemorate the dead of the First World War.

The main entrance gates to Netherhall mansion were decorated with laurel leaves on the occasion of the marriage of Dorothy Elizabeth Pocklington Senhouse, elder daughter of Mrs and the late Mr H. Senhouse, to Joseph Walter Scott Plummer of Sunderland Hall, Selkirk, on 6 April 1904.

A wedding photograph from the Senhouse-Plummer wedding in 1906. The bride Dorothy is in the centre with her young brother, Roger Henry Pocklington Senhouse, the page-boy. The groom, Joseph Plummer stands on the right. The bridesmaids were Blanche (Dorothy's sister) and Miss Holland-Hibbert (a cousin), and the bride was given away by her brother Guy Joseph Pocklington Senhouse.

Netherhall, the Senhouse family home since the reign of Henry VIII. Over the years it has undergone several extensions. It was last occupied by Col. Guy Pocklington Senhouse until his death in 1952. It then passed to his younger brother Roger who lived and worked in London. When Roger died in 1960 it was suffering from vandalism and eventually became a complete ruin. It was demolished in the 1970s, leaving only the old peel tower standing today.

A rear view of Netherhall, showing the weir which formed the boating lake. It also shows the ivy-clad peel tower, the oldest part of the mansion, and to the right the ballroom with the library above.

The Netherhall beagle pack on the front lawn, c. 1902.

Local farmer James Messenger of Camp Farm, outside Netherhall, driving one of the Senhouse carriages around the grounds, c. 1958. On board are some members of the Maryport archery club at a fund raising fête for guide dogs for the blind.

The front portico to Netherhall with the Roman artefacts collected by the Senhouse family over the centuries. The collection is now displayed in the Roman Senhouse Museum, formerly the 'Battery' on the sea brows.

John Huddart with his horse and cart in the grounds of Netherhall, at one of the annual fêtes held in the park. John lost his leg in the First World War but overcame his handicap and sold fresh fish around Maryport.

Staff in the kitchen at Netherhall, c. 1910.

Gardeners cutting the rear lawn at Netherhall.

The old toll cottage at Ellengrove, c. 1891. At this time it was occupied by William McHendry and his family. It ceased to be a tollgate towards the end of the 1860s.

Ellengrove Villa was built around 1899 by Tom S. McGraa on the site of the old toll cottage. Tom was overseer for the Crosscanonby and Netherton parishes; he had previously been a boot and shoe manufacturer at 40 Senhouse Street, Maryport.

The opening ceremony of the Ellengrove Laundry in 1909, performed by Lord Muncaster, here seen seated beside Sir Wilfred Lawson. Mrs F. Senhouse had the idea of funding the laundry to give young ladies the opportunity to train as maids before going into service.

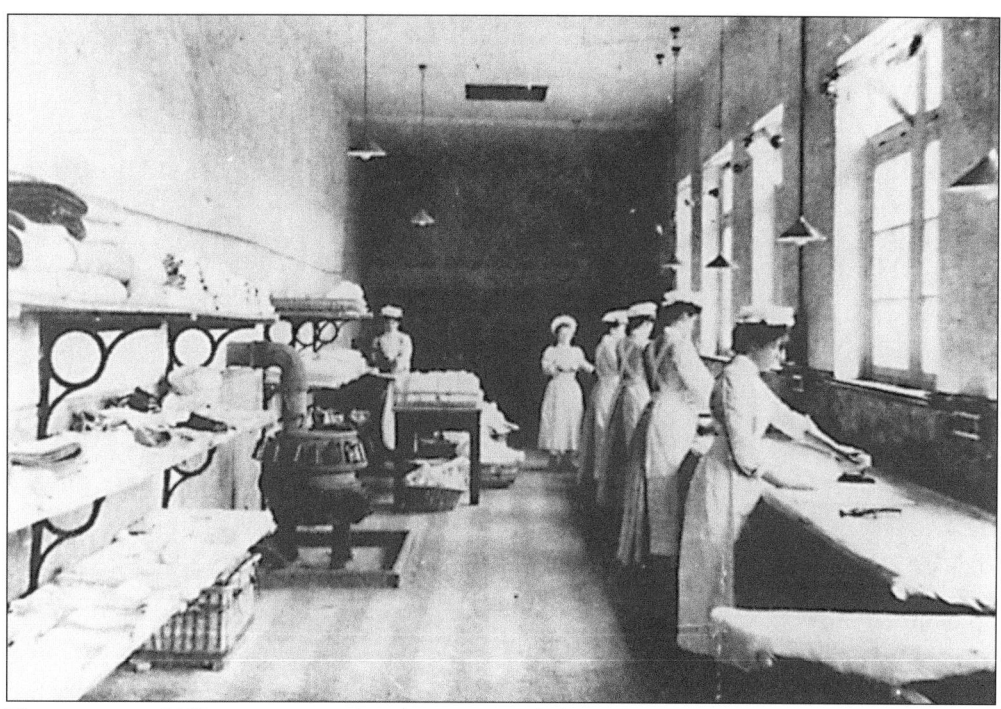

The interior of Ellengrove Laundry shows young ladies who were under the supervision of a resident matron. The laundry also had living quarters for the girls. It closed in the late 1920s.

The River Ellen Bridge Cottage, a former toll cottage, at the junction of the Mealpot and Netherton roads.

A view of the Ellenborough New Road at Netherton. This part of Maryport was built in the last quarter of the nineteenth century to ease the housing shortage in the rapidly growing town.

The clergy and choir of All Souls' church, Netherton, c. 1906.

The houses known as Ghyll and Chagford Villas at Ellenbourgh. The Chagford Villas were the second phase of this row. The Ghyll was built in the 1890s and Chagford Villas were built by John Ellis, builder of John Street, around 1905.

Looking down from Ellenborough onto the old reservoir and allotments in front of the terraced houses of Netherton.

A gentlemen's trip stops for another passenger at Hayborough Lodge gates in 1927. Ritchie's motor engineers of John Street owned the charabanc.

Ewanrigg Hall at Ellenbourgh is said to be named after Ewen, a northern king. In the nineteenth century the Christian family of the Isle of Man were the owners of the mansion.

Six
Grasslot and the Railway

An early print of the station and engine sheds of the Maryport and Carlisle Railway at Grasslot. The construction of the line began in 1837 and the first section to Aspatria was completed by 1840. With the opening of this line, it greatly improved the transport of coal from local pits down to the harbour at Maryport.

The Maryport and Carlisle No. 25 engine, built by Beyer Peacock in 1878, seen outside the engine shed at Grasslot. Behind the engine can be seen the scaffolding for the construction of the sand furnace chimney.

A group of M&C engineers in 1916. A large number of men trained at Grasslot eventually went on to become either ships' engineers or motor mechanics.

The Station Hotel at Grasslot was built in the nineteenth century to accommodate passengers on the M&C Railway. This photograph shows Tom Woodward standing outside his hotel.

Grasslot signal box on the dock junction of the south line to divert trains onto the Elizabeth and Senhouse Docks.

The Solway Ironworks, Grasslot. this was built on land owned by Humphrey P Senhouse. The furnace was fired for the first time in 1871, and the company flourished. When profits began to fluctuate around 1894 work was suspended, but two years later production resumed under Charles Cammell & Co. of Sheffield. Before 1909 it became part of the Workington Iron Steel Co. and it finally closed down in 1927. The buildings were demolished in 1939.

Ironworkers at Grasslot. John Brinicombe on the left arrived in Maryport with his wife and family in around 1878, moving into a house on Mandle Street, Grasslot, that was owned by the Solway Ironworks.

The Kraus family were Czech refugees who had fled to England to escape German occupation and formed the Hornflowa factory in 1938. They brought with them their process of using powdered horn and resin for the manufacture of buttons. They started production in a small unit, which later became part of the Bata shoe factory on the Solway Industrial Estate. In 1942 the first part of this purpose-built factory was completed; at the same time the company was joined by Dr Herzberg, an Austrian refugee, who had been a banker. By 1947, with demand for buttons rising, the factory had doubled in size.

Lawson Wood, a successful commercial artist, was commissioned by Hornflowa Ltd to paint a series of advertising posters. This shows one of a series of six advertising their buttons.

This shop at No. 1 Collins Terrace, Grasslot (seen here in around 1913), was licensed to sell beer but not spirits, and became known as the 'Jerry' or 'Jug and Bottle'. As well as beer it also sold groceries. The last occupier was Mrs Irene Neri and the shop closed on New Year's Eve 1976. The shop was demolished a short time afterwards to make room for road improvements.

The flooded main road at Collins Terrace, c. 1960. Flooding was a common occurrence for many years until the road, and the beck which flooded, were altered.

A street party in Collins Terrace in 1953 to celebrate the coronation of Queen Elizabeth II.

In 1920 the Government introduced and implemented the Miners' Welfare Act. The miners' welfare fund was financed partly by the Government and partly by mine owners, with a levy of one penny per ton of coal, which was later raised to twopence. This was used to provide sports and recreation facilities. The Grasslot Miners' Welfare Club, shown here, was opened in 1926.

The decision to build a hospital in Maryport was taken in July 1901 with the support of Mrs Florence Catherine P. Senhouse. The foundation stones were laid in April 1902, and Mrs Senhouse opened the Victoria Cottage Hospital in January 1903.

The foundation stone for the Edward VII Memorial Ward being laid by Mrs Florence Senhouse, assisted by her daughter Mrs Blanche Clutterbuck, in 1911.

The new Victoria Cottage Hospital in Ewanrigg Road, showing the interior of the men's ward.

Miss Langcake with her pupils in the playground of Grasslot School, 1921.

Looking from the bridge over the M&C railway line at Grasslot, towards the old blast furnace and C. Minshaw's Furnace Sawmill on Mill Street, c. 1900.

The old blast furnace at Mill Street, built in 1752 on land leased from Humphrey Senhouse. The furnace was built by a group of businessmen and designed to operate on coke. The air came from bellows driven by a water wheel. The furnace continued until 1783 when it was put up for sale, because at times there was insufficient water for the wheel. Unfortunately no purchaser was found, so the furnace was taken over by H. Senhouse and remained idle until its demolition in 1963.

Looking down from Mote Hill onto the slaughterhouse on Mill Street, c. 1957. The bus station and Greggain's petrol station are behind.

The Solway Garage filling station, built in 1950/51.

Maryport bus station in Curzon Street, *c.* 1955. The site belonged to the Cumberland Motor Services who leased it in 1934 and built the first garage two years later. The garage was extended in 1942 and the site altered and covered over in 1960. CMS were taken over by Stagecoach in 1996 and the garage was sold and demolished shortly afterwards.

Looking north along Curzon Street, *c.* 1905. The houses on the left were built around 1888.

Maryport railway station, opened in 1860. The stationmaster's house is on the left and on the right are the clock tower and the offices and boardroom of the Maryport & Carlisle Railway Company. The clock tower and boardroom were demolished in 1960 and the remaining buildings went in 1972.

The station and platform with the M&C's old No. 19 engine, built by the company in 1867, seen heading north with carriages. The engine ran until 1914.

Looking along Station Street towards the railway station, c. 1906. The Baptist church is on the right.

The Trinity Baptist church in Station Street, which was built in 1891 to replace the old church in High Street which is now the Masonic Hall.

A group of local Marines outside the Baptist church in 1914/15. They have just arrived from Carlisle in a taxi for a few days' leave. They had taken part in the siege of Antwerp.

Looking from the Mealpot along Station Street, towards the Co-op buildings on Curzon Street, c. 1910. On the right is Bettoney's Granville Commercial Hotel, which later became the Granville, a gentlemen's club.

General Booth, founder of the Salvation Army, arriving in Station Street in August 1905 during his tour of Cumberland. After a brief stop at Flimby, he arrived in Maryport in the late morning and addressed the crowd in the Baptist church. After the meeting General Booth was invited to have lunch with Wilfred Hine at Camp Hill before continuing his tour to Wigton.

A Maryport carnival procession entering Curzon Street from Station Street, c. 1935.

Seven
Sport and Leisure

The bowling green and the new athletic ground on what had been known as the cricket ground on the Mealpot. The new ground was opened on 23 June 1901 with a series of cycle races promoted by the Maryport Wheelers Cycle Club. The Athletic Association had constructed a 440-yard grass cycle track and grandstand. This replaced a smaller track which had been created in the 1880s, situated where the present tennis courts are now, beside the bowling green.

Maryport bowling green and pavilion, 1924. The club was formed in September 1878 with Mirehouse Wilson as the first chairman.

Local ironmonger Mirehouse Wilson about to bowl in around 1910. he was president of the Maryport club for twenty-three years.

Maryport Solway Bicycle Club members on Netherhall Road with their penny-farthing bicycles, c. 1880.

Local rider Cliff Thompson just beating two Barrow riders in the final of the 1-mile cycle handicap. This was the first meeting in June 1901 on the new track; the Maryport Wheelers Cycle Club sponsored the meeting.

A Maryport tradesmen's football team in front of the grandstand on the Athletic Ground, c. 1908.

The Maryport ladies' football team, c. 1918. The majority of these young ladies were employed at Williamson's tannery in Nelson Street.

Bellman Dick Howe of Maryport. Dick was born in 1846 at Parsonby Brow Top; he had a varied career, having been first employed as a pit boy at Brayton Domain Colliery and later as a farmworker. Eventually moving to Maryport, by 1891 he had established himself as a bellman and that year he was invited to Grasmere Sports Day to announce the competitors. Being such a success, Dick was bellman for the next thirty years. He always spoke in a broad Cumberland dialect, confusing locals and visitors alike. Dick followed Cumberland and Westmorland-style wrestling and would be heard to call 'If thoo doesn't cum inta t'ring thoo'll be blawn oot.' Dick died in 1923, having been the first gardener to look after the Memorial Gardens at Netherhall corner.

The bowling green and rugby ground, which had replaced the cycle track, c. 1955. The venue was now known as the athletic ground.

Local MP Fred Peart opens the new bowling green clubhouse in January 1975, surrounded by some local council officials and club members.

Monty Irving and his Jesters Jazz Band on the cricket ground. This was one of the local jazz bands, which entertained at fêtes and carnivals.

Maryport's first brass band was formed in 1890 and was known as the Town Band. This photograph shows the Solway Silver Band in around 1937 outside the Battery, which was its meeting place. After the Second World War the band changed its name to the Maryport Albion Band, and moved to rooms in Kirkby Street to practice.

Maryport Rugby Union team outside Netherhall, c. 1894. Over the years the Maryport team won a large number of trophies. In 1898 the County Rugby Union Committee suspended one of the Maryport players in his absence and without any club official present to represent him. Unable to come to any agreement with the governing committee, the Maryport club called a meeting in the Coffee Tavern to discuss the suspension. Eventually a vote was taken and it was unanimously decided to leave the Rugby Union and join the recently formed Northern Union, later to become known as the Rugby League.

The Brookland Rovers Northern Union team in 1905. They were intermediate team winners of the Cumberland Junior Shield, beating Whitehaven Recreation 3-0 in the final, by scoring a try in extra time.

Maryport's cricket XI, who became Cumberland senior league champions for 1936. From left to right, back row: J. Bayliss (scorer) E.D. Smith, (vice captain) W.S. Carter, R. Skelton, J.A. Henderson, J.S. Nichol, J.J. Hine (umpire). Middle row: W. Abbott (honorary treasurer), R. Arnold (chairman), H.O. Marsden (captain), W. Potter (vice chairman), R.E. Fisher (honorary secretary). Front row: R.W. Garret, J. Haile, J. Jefferson, T. Gibson.

The first Ellenfoot Rugby Union team. This club was formed in March 1950, introducing rugby union back into Maryport after a spell of fifty-two years. A group of local rugby players who had been playing for neighbouring clubs met in the Prince Regent Inn and unanimously agreed to form a team. A fixture was arranged with Workington Zebras at the end of the 1949/50 season. Their first full season, 1950/51, was a success; they fielded two teams and reached the Cumberland Cup final, only to be beaten 11-0 by Keswick.

The Bata shoe company's netball team, c. 1959. From left to right, back row: Gladys Wood, -?-, -?-, Jean Orr, Martha Easterbrook. Front row: Mary Shimmings, Eleanor Richardson, Audrey Southwell.

Ellenborough Jolly Boys Jazz Band, c. 1963. This group, led by Billy Bryce, was formed to enter a carnival in the 1950s using anything that would make a noise! From this modest beginning they managed to acquire some instruments and persuaded some local musicians to join them. They then became well known, giving concerts and travelling to carnivals all over the North of England, and raising money for charities, especially for the old folks of Ellenborough.

St Mary's Church Girls' Friendly Society, 1927. They were the winners of the Diocesan Country Dancing competition at Newcastle, and are seen with their dancing teacher Miss Amies.

The jazz band from the Artillery Arms public house in Catherine Street. John Eddy Shimmings leads the band up Shipping Brow in the Maryport carnival, 1959.

Rose Queen Marion Dockray with her attendants in one of the last Grasslot carnivals, *c.* 1949. From left to right: Mary Shimmings, Marjorie Williams, Marion Dockray, Ann Murray, Valerie Wharton.

The Down Street 'Belles' taking advantage of a hot spell and having a dip in the sea on Maryport shore, *c.* 1930.

Eight
Flimby

William Gibson, the deputy at Risehow Colliery, stands on the left with Tom Stephenson, the miners' leader, addressing the miners at Flimby about new working methods. The Cumberland coal mines were the oldest and most backward in the country, with the miners amongst the poorest. This led them to take part in the hunger march for better conditions and the abolition of means testing. The march began in Workington in the winter of 1934. The Second World War brought about a national shortage of coal and a mining engineer, James Adam Nimmo, was sent to Cumberland by the government to become General Manager of the coal mines on the west coast. His job was to modernize the mining methods to increase production. In 1947 the mines were nationalized and Risehow Colliery eventually closed in January 1966.

The main road leading south through Fothergill, showing the level crossing. The railway line led to the pit and the engine shed of the Risehow Colliery, Coking and By-Products Company. By 1924 the United Steel Companies had bought a share in the Risehow Colliery.

Risehow Pit junction signal box on the LNWR line. This shows the signal and rail staff who had gathered for a colleague's leaving presentation in 1925. Thomas Clark Wilkinson (second from the right at the front) was the signalman. The man at the top of the steps was George Wise, a plate layer; and third from left at the back is Jim Pearson, who left the company to move to London, eventually becoming the chief inspector at Euston station.

The bowling green on the south side of Flimby Lodge, with the tennis pavilion in the background, c. 1924.

Members of the tennis club outside the pavilion in 1915. The tennis club was formed in the 1870s.

Standing in six acres of land, Flimby Lodge was set back from the main road between Fothergill and Flimby. It was formerly a girls' boarding school. In 1886 it was purchased by the Cockermouth Union and had room for around 100 children. A vagrant ward and hospital with sixteen beds was added in 1887. By 1896 the vagrant wards were occupied by thirty-five boys and eighteen girls. Isaac Irving was the superintendent and his wife Sarah was matron at the Lodge in 1910.

Flimby carnival day in 1960, with Billy Bryce leading the Ellenborough Jolly Boys Jazz Band in the procession from Fothergill into the village. The spoil heap of Risehow Colliery can be seen in the background.

Flimby Board School was built in 1876, enlarged several times and by 1901 had room for 600 children. William Parkinson was headmaster; he occupied the schoolhouse to the right. By the 1940s the schoolhouse had become the village policeman's residence.

Flimby Girls' School netball team. 1923. The headmistress, Miss Sarah Hodgson, is on the right.

121

Flimby Ambulance Corps outside the school in Rye Hill Road in 1897. Captain J.W. Davidson is seated in the centre.

A view along Rye Hill Road in 1922, with the Wesleyan Chapel on the left, which was built in 1858 and closed in 1950. The members then moved to the Primitive Chapel on West Lane and became the United Methodists.

The Flimby Male Voice Choir in 1937 with their trophies. In the centre behind the large rose bowl is Thomas Clark Wilkinson, who was their conductor for forty-three years.

Flimby Band was formed in 1878 as a drum and fife band, becoming a brass band in 1889. This photograph shows Flimby Saxhorn Silver Band in 1950, outside the Wesleyan Chapel Hall after winning the cup at Seaton. J. Hurst was the president (with the cup) and J. Robley the conductor (third from the right at the front).

The Brow, looking down towards the Wheatsheaf Inn at the bottom, c. 1907. Behind the cottages on the left was the Primitive Methodist chapel, until the new chapel was built on West Lane in 1927.

Looking up Flimby Brow, c. 1924. The first building on the left was Maggie Scott's fish and chip shop; further up on the right was Simpson's grocery shop which later became the top Co-operative store.

St Nicholas' church, whose registers date back to 1696. The church was under the chapelry of Camerton until 1546. In 1794 it was rebuilt on the site of the old church and was restored in 1862 to hold a congregation of 194.

The view down Brook Street. The wooden building on the left was originally Harry Tinnion's Billiard Hall; it became the Flimby Ambulance Corps centre in 1927, when the Miners' Welfare Club opened. A young Dick Atkinson can be seen on the right wearing breeches.

The Maryport Co-operative Industrial Society No. 5 branch in Chapel Street, which was opened in 1892. It was built by local builders Messrs Smith and Marshall as part of the society's policy of opening stores in the surrounding mining villages.

Looking along Station Road, with the steps leading up to the railway station on the left, c. 1922. On the right is Tom and Bessie Coulthard's newsagents with Johnny Peel's hairdressers further along.

126

The view towards Station Road, with the railway station on the left and Westfield Terrace on the right. In the nineteenth and early twentieth centuries, Flimby was a popular bathing place. It had a wide area of grass above the shingle used as a picnic and games area.

Looking up Brook Street from Station Road, with the Princess Royal Inn on the right. Mrs Margaret Twentyman was the licensee in 1904.

Walter Stackwood came to Flimby with his wife and three daughters in 1933 from South Africa He opened a market garden on the beach side of the Maryport to Workington road. To this he built a shop, café, concert hall and amusement arcade, calling the complex Long and Small, which he named after the property he had occupied in South Africa.

The monkey house at Long and Small, which held two pet monkeys, Come-Come and Go-Go. In the background of this 1938 view are the beach and swings, with the LMS railway line from Maryport to Workington at the rear of the Long and Small garage.